Instant Borders & Frames

GRAPHICS WORLD

CAMERA-READY ART FOR DESIGNERS & PRINTERS

ISBN 0-86250-015-X

**The Graphic Communications Centre Ltd.,
Bernard House, Granville Road,
Maidstone, Kent ME14 2BJ. England.
Telephone 0622 675324**

Introducing the Graphics World Instant Art library

This book you are now holding is just one volume in an ever expanding library of ready-to-use and commercially orientated illustrations and graphics published by Graphics World, Britain's leading graphic communications magazine and publisher.

The Graphics World Instant Art library has many benefits to offer a wide variety of people throughout the international visual communications industry. Wherever illustrations and graphics to a high professional standard are required quickly and at minimum cost the Instant Art library is the answer.

These books are principally intended for use by professional designers and paste-up artists in the graphics and reprographics industries but can also be a great asset to anyone skilled or novice who has to prepare artwork for any kind of publicity, editorial design, displays, overhead projection slides, posters, presentation etc.

Having purchased this book the art material it contains is yours to use within the restrictions of our copyright (see previous page) and without any further payment. If you have commissioned any illustration recently you will have already appreciated the true value of this Instant Art book — a single illustration will have almost certainly cost you more than the price of this book.

At the time this particular book was published the Instant Art library consisted of eight volumes but this is only the beginning of a very comprehensive system. To keep fully up to date send in your name and address to Graphics World at the address shown on the title page and we will keep you right up to date with all our new books.

Each of the books in this library have 160 pages of art presented in a case-bound format designed to meet most end user requirements, as the books can either be kept intact or if you wish the individual pages can be removed and placed in a standard ring binder.

In consideration of the purchasers who do not have the facility of a reprographic camera to reduce and enlarge art, some of the illustrations are supplied in two or three sizes. Designers with access to a reprographic camera, however, can reproduce directly from the book using a photographic print as a paste-up original, so avoiding the need to mutilate the book.

The illustrations, graphics and photographs featured in this library offer you unlimited creative opportunity. In addition to the wide variety of subject matter, style of illustration and graphic ideas, all the art can be personalised and customised using one or more of the many photographic or mechanical techniques available to today's designer. With a reprographic camera art can be enlarged, reduced, turned to negative, tinted etc. all in a matter of minutes.

To make the most of your investment familiarise yourself with the contents of the book and let the art available influence your ideas rather than your ideas be frustrated by the

Instant Art Book One
ISBN 0-86250-010-9

Instant Art Books 1 and 2 are the basis of the system and feature general illustrations and graphics including people, faces, places, cartoons, headings, merchandise, seasonal art, animals and other attention-compelling graphics. Ideal for the first time buyer and general art user.

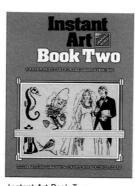

Instant Art Book Two
ISBN 0-86250-018-4

This volume is a further selection of general material for advertising and editorial applications. All the art is of U.K. origin, and professionally executed by our own experienced technical, figure and cartoon illustrators, lettering and graphic designers.

Instant Symbols & Graphics
ISBN 0-86250-013-3

Modern communications often rely on symbols, to direct, inform and identify. This book features over 1 400 different graphic symbols and illustrations ideal for use in newspapers, magazines, handbooks, sign systems and general graphics — or used as business logos. Ideal also as a reference source.

Instant Borders & Frames
ISBN 0-86250-015-X

A collection of hundreds of different borders, frames, banners, corner pieces and flourishes in every conceivable shape, size and style to cater for every type of design job. The potential applications are endless, particularly in the production of vouchers, coupons, brochures and press advertisements.

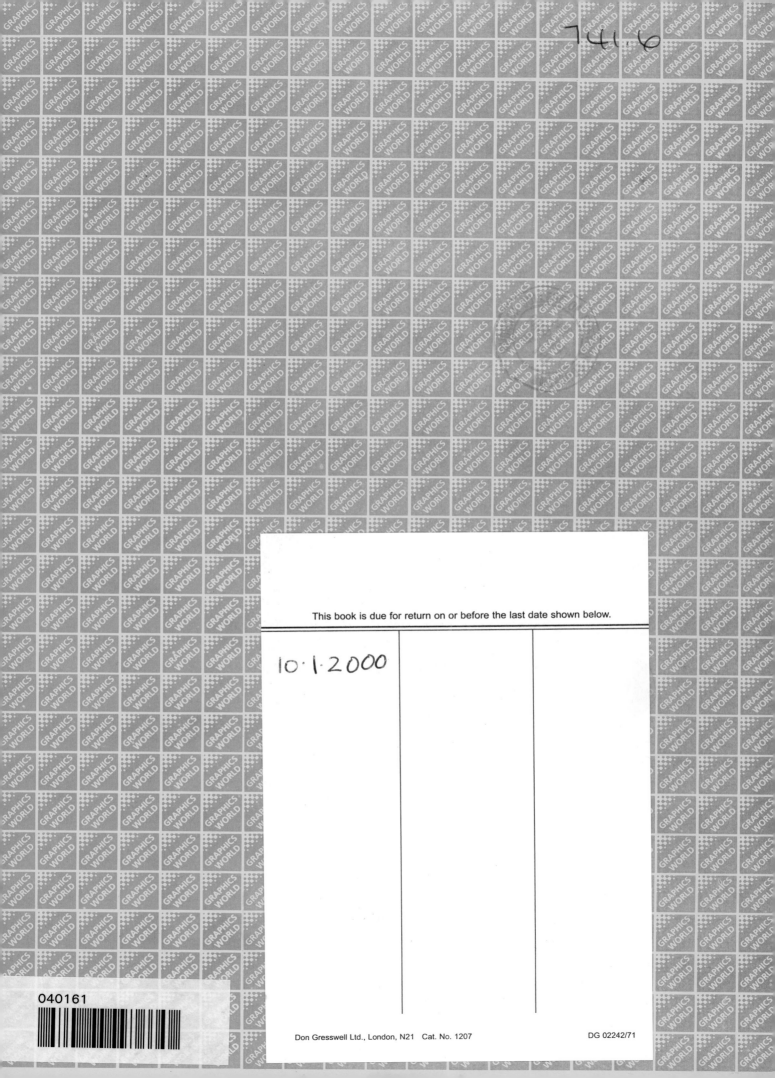

Instant Borders & Frames

GRAPHICS WORLD

Film assembly and platemaking by
Abacus Reproduction Studios, Maidstone, Kent.

Printed by
Penshurst Press Ltd., Tunbridge Wells, Kent.

Bound by
Mansell (Bookbinders) Ltd., Witham Essex.

lack of applicable art. Obviously the more volumes you invest in the greater range of art you will have to select from. It is also very important to familiarise yourself with all the techniques available today and the best way to do this is to invest in our book 'Instant Graphic Techniques', which has been produced in conjunction with Agfa-Gevaert and fully demonstrates all the possibilities of both the Agfa Copyproof System and the Graphics World Instant Art library. Used with a little imagination the art in this book will save you many hours of work, add to your overall design efficiency and profitability and ensure a professional finish to every design project.

Instant Art in action

Illustrated to the right are just a few example of 'Instant Art' in action. Leaflets, programmes, catalogues, cards, press advertisements, packaging, etc., the possibilities are endless the only limiting factor is your creative imagination — and don't forget when you come up with an unusual application or create something really special, keep us in the picture — send Graphics World a review or sample.

Instant Colour Art
ISBN 0-86250-017-6

A unique collection of full colour and two colour illustrations and photographs illustrated in full colour and also supplied as 100# dot-for-dot separations. Ideal for magazine, brochure and catalogue covers — just make four line exposures and you'll have full colour separations at a fraction of the cost of conventional colour separations.

Instant Archive Art
ISBN 0-86250-021-4

A specially researched and selected collection of old engravings and period art to meet the needs of the advertiser and graphic designer. Every piece of art featured has been carefully chosen for relevance and reproductive qualities.

Instant Photo Art
ISBN 0-86250-011-7

For that special effect, photographic art this is the book you need — a superb collection of 160 photographs all carefully reproduced using special effect and posterisation techniques. Subject matter is extremely varied — ideal for advertisements and cover designs.

Instant Food Art
ISBN 0-86250-016-8

This is a specialist volume packed with art for everyone involved in catering or food merchandising and includes four colour and two colour separations — plus hundreds of line drawings and graphics including: meats, vegetables, fruits, cakes, food dishes, people, scenes and graphics perfect for supermarket press advertising, point of sale displays, packaging and promotion offers.

Making the most of Instant Art

There are many occasions when art selected from the Instant Art library will be just what you need, but there will also be many other occasions when art will have to be re-sized or modified slightly in some way to meet your exact requirements. The professional designer, understandably, will also be looking for opportunities to use his creative flair by adding his personal interpretation to illustrations and graphics taken from the library.

Today's successful graphic designer must learn to blend traditional art and design skills with creative technology, materials and processes. Instant Art can be used in isolation but its true potential is only fully realised when used with a little imagination in conjunction with other graphic aids.

In order to explain and demonstrate many of the current techniques being used by leading designers particularly in conjunction with Instant Art, Graphics World have published a special book called 'Instant Graphic Techniques' with the full co-operation of Agfa-Gevaert, the world's leading manufacturer and supplier of studio process cameras and associated photo-chemical systems and products.

'Instant Graphic Techniques' is in fact just one of many professional step-by-step books being produced by Graphics World in conjunction with major manufacturers and provides both the experienced and novice designer with a mine of information, hints and tips plus creative ideas.

▶ The Copyproof system is the simple, fast and economical way to reproduce in enlarged, reduced, positive or negative form Instant Art originals.

▼ An Agfa-Gevaert Repromaster 1 000 in action. A compact process camera of this nature or access to such a repro service is a great advantage to any Instant Art user.

There are 96 pages of lavishly illustrated text and 72 pages of Instant Art selected from the eight volumes. No designer or Instant Art user wishing to make the most of their Instant Art investment should be without this fundamental guide to graphic techniques which includes useful information on such subjects as: The process camera, processors and processing techniques; the Copyproof and Copychrome systems; equipping a modern darkroom,

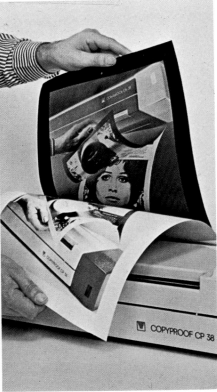

equipping an efficient studio; preparing, presenting and preserving originals; scaling art for reproduction; basic line work techniques; enlarging and reducing images, producing mirror and negative images; multiple exposure and step-and-repeat techniques; line conversions; how to produce high quality halftones and special effect halftones; special effect screens; posterisation techniques; over-printing and reversing out type; producing continuous tone images; ghosting techniques, screening and tinting techniques, complex tint work; solarisation effects; special effects and experimental graphics; two colour images such as duotones and two colour photo conversions, two colour tinting, textures and mechanical tints; producing overhead transparency slides with Copychrome; full colour

tinting and overlays, colour proofing, full colour photo conversions and many other ideas and applications including making the most of Instant Art dot-for-dot colour separations.

Never befor has so much useful information been packed into one book. If you really want to make the most of your skills and investment in Instant Art it is essential that this book is added to your reference library.

Part of the comprehensive Copyproof and Copychrome system which is fully explained and demonstrated in the book Instant Graphic Techniques illustrated to the right. The extensive range of materials mix and match in conjunction with other materials to give the designer hundreds of different creative options in both black and white and colour for each different piece of Instant Art.

Instant Graphic Techniques
WITH INSTANT ART & AGFA-GEVAERT

INCLUDES 72 PAGES OF CAMERA-READY ART

1

8

Use a little imagination...

With Instant Art the usual can be turned into the unusual in a matter of moments. Use a little imagination coupled with an appreciation and understanding of basic graphic techniques and what was just a basic graphic illustration can become a compelling graphic image. Here are just a few ideas to get you thinking. (1) original illustration. (2) negative image. (3) mirror image. (4) enlarged and cropped. (5) step and repeated. (6) screen tinted. (7) simple modification. (8) special effect screening. (9) full colour tinting.

FILLING YOU IN
The design and production techniques behind a Brian Sanders illustration

BY JAMES CRAIG

Other useful Graphics World publications and services

Graphics World the publishers of this book, offer to designers and everyone with an interest in graphic communications a service unrivalled by any other publisher in Europe.

Graphics World magazine, available on a worldwide basis for an annual subscription of £10 per annum (1981/82 rate) keeps you right up to date with the latest developments in graphic design and graphic communications equipment, materials, processes, techniques and services.

Graphics World also operate the largest direct mail graphics book service in Europe, importing and exporting books on all contemporary aspects of graphics, design, advertising and printing to individuals, companies and educational establishments throughout the world.

To obtain a complimentary sample copy of Graphics World magazine and our current book catalogue please write to:—

**The Graphic Communications Centre Ltd.
Bernard House, Granville Road,
Maidstone, Kent ME14 2BJ. England.
Telephone 0622 675324**

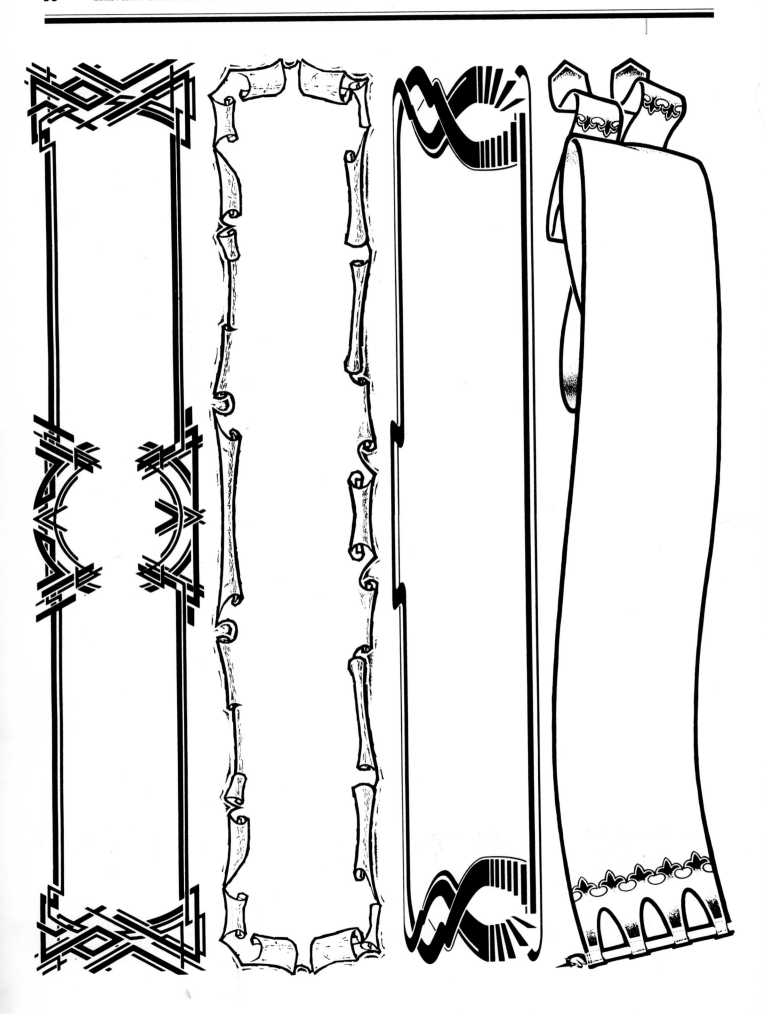

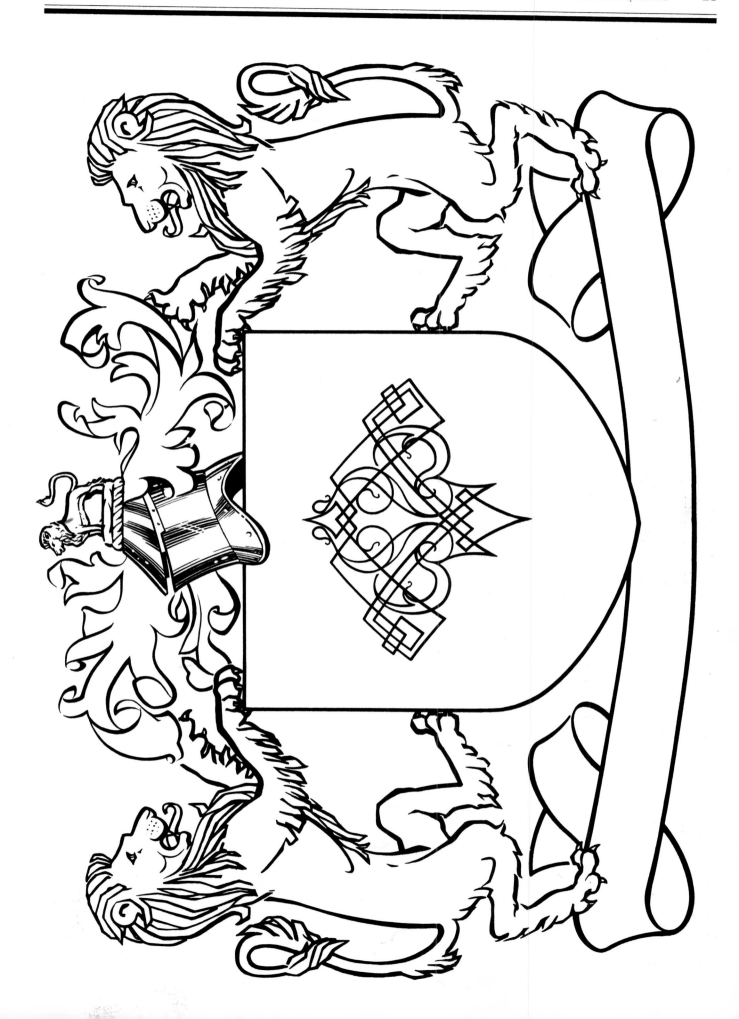

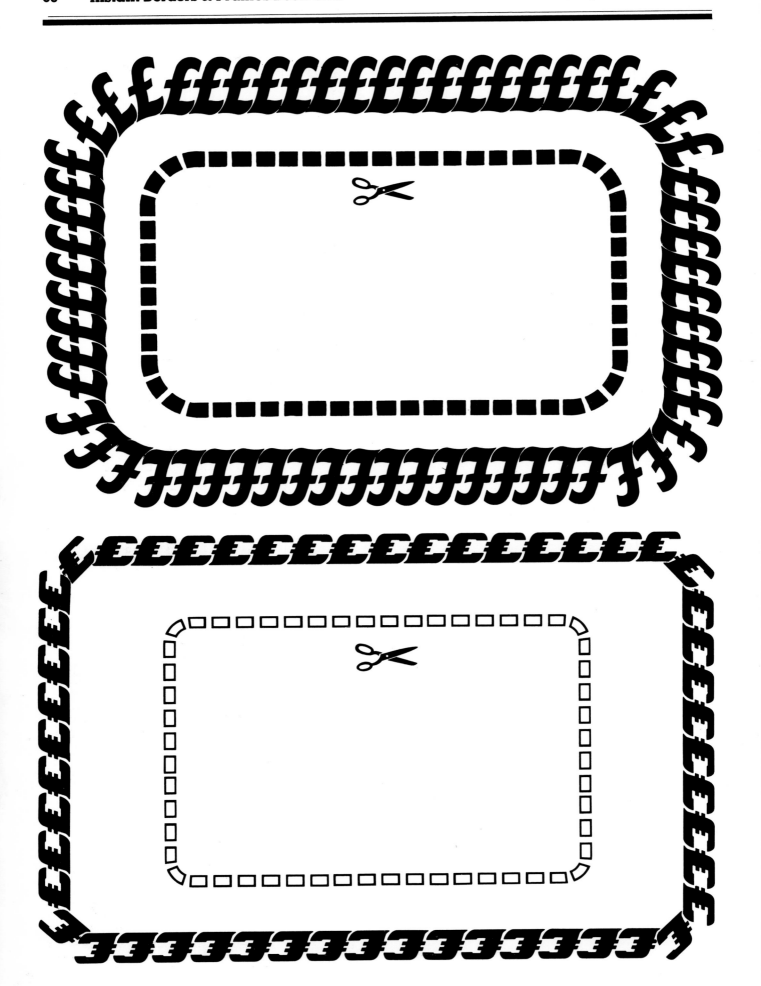

Instant Borders & Frames Book One

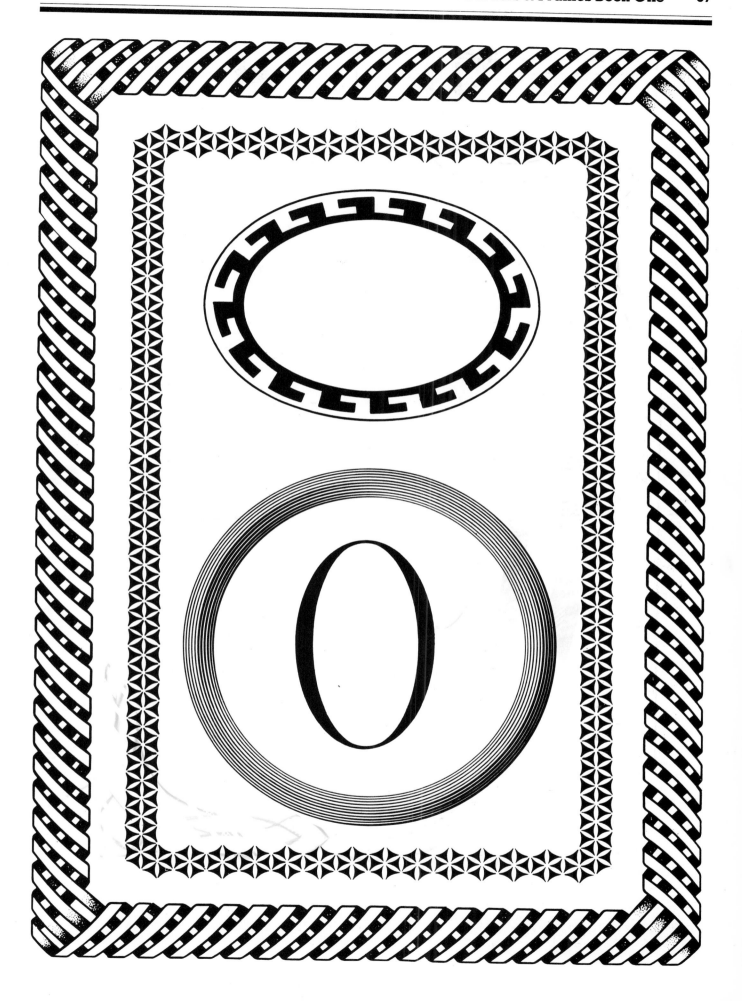

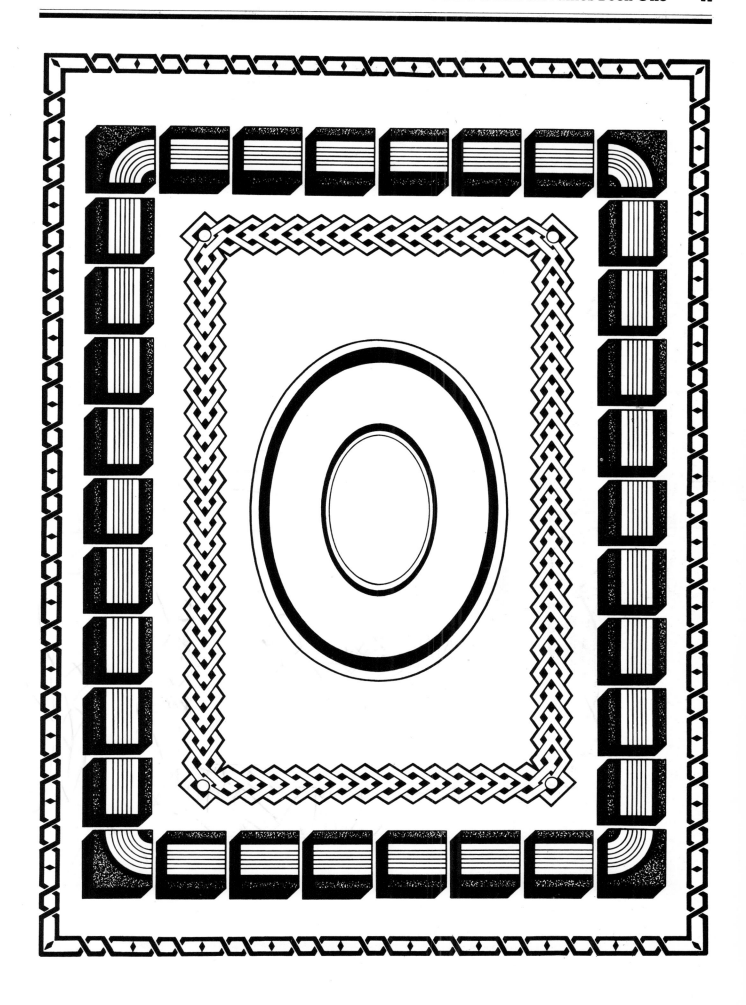

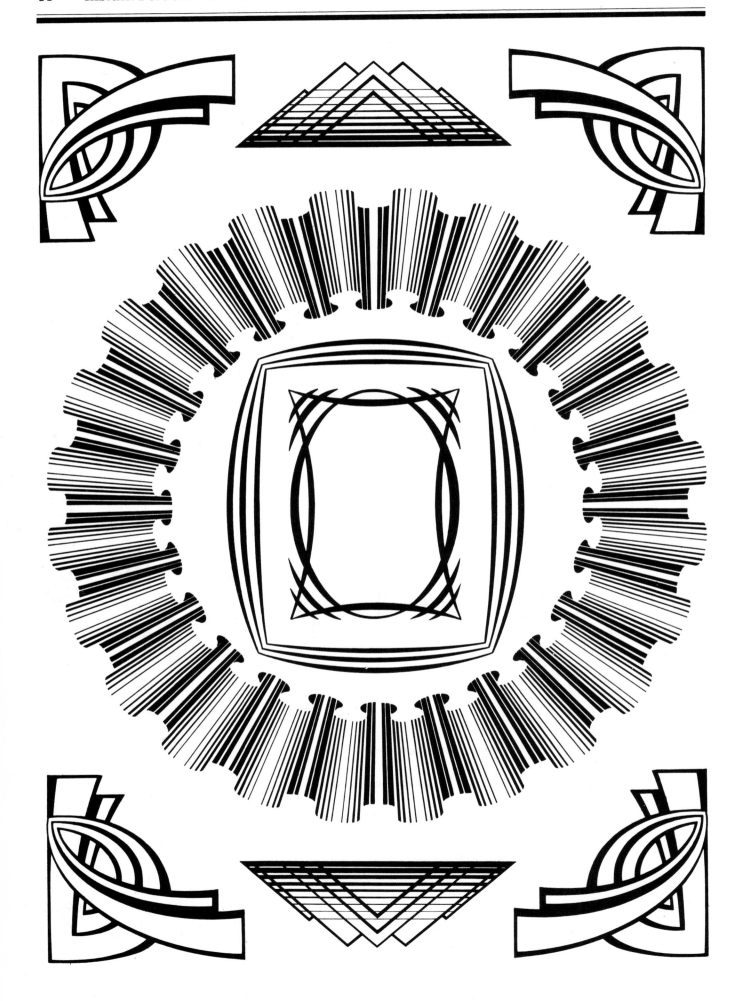

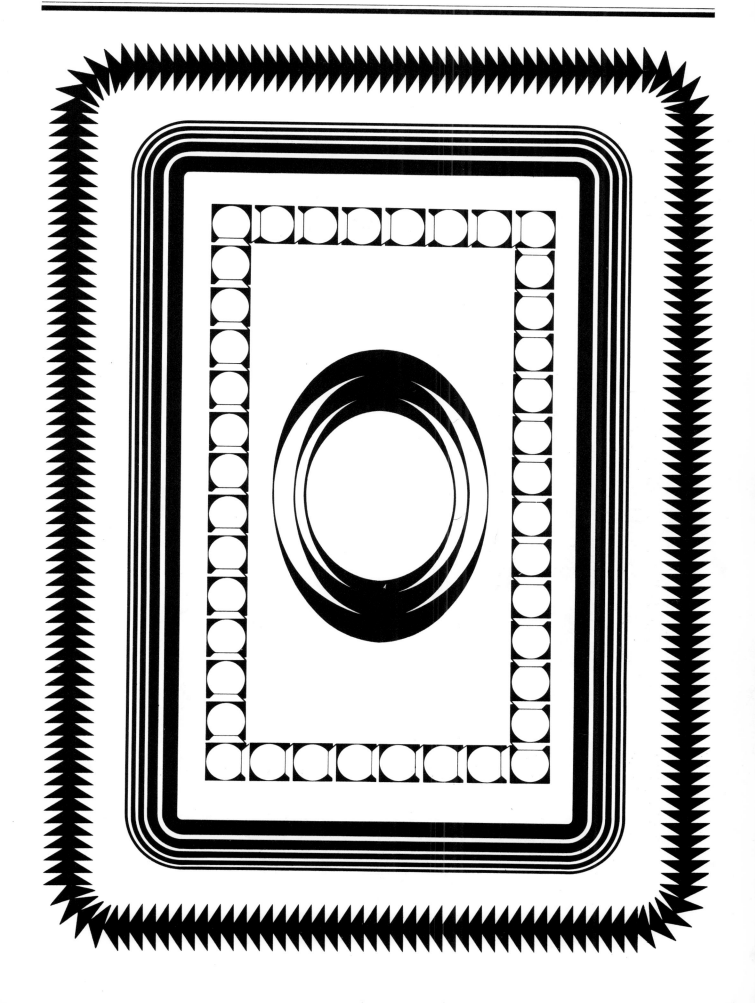

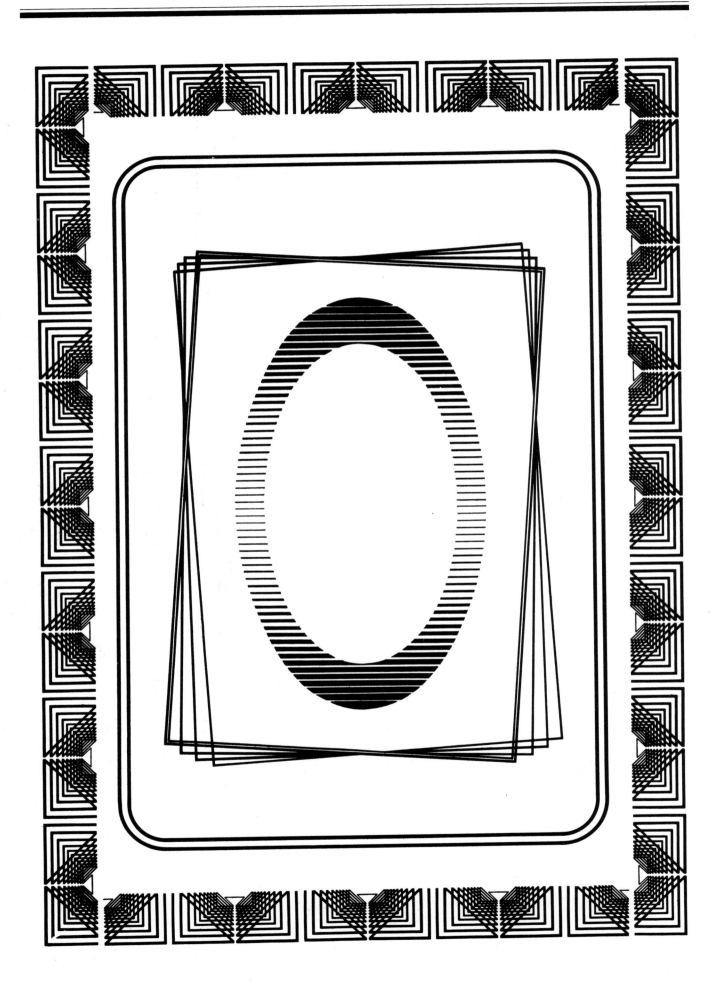

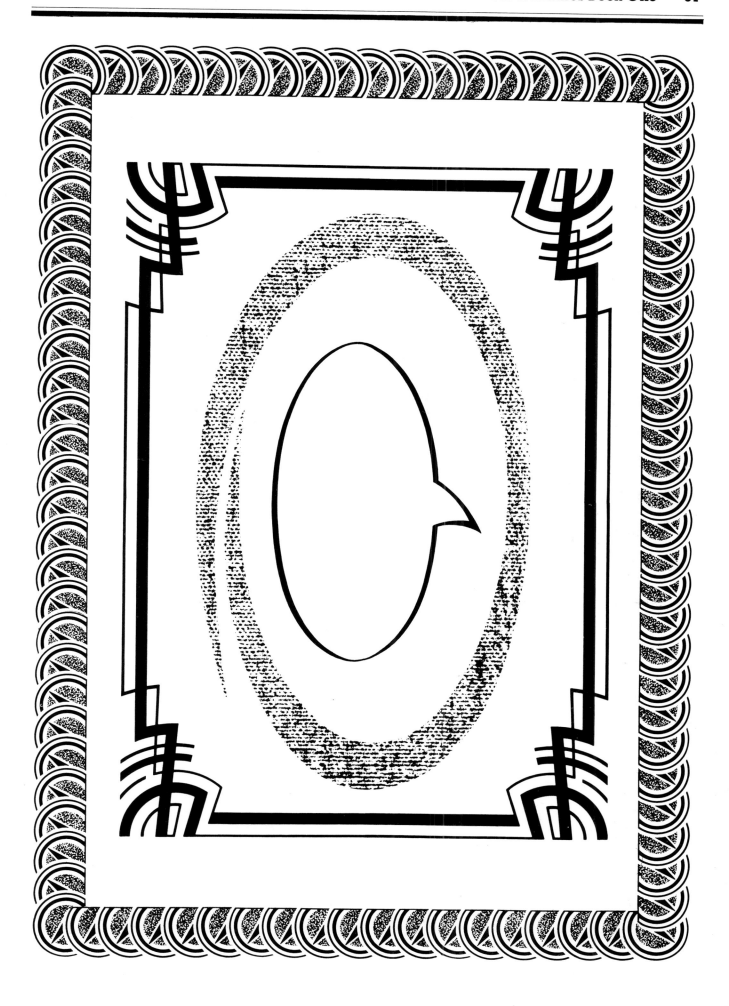

TIME IS MONEY...

GOLF TOURNAMENT

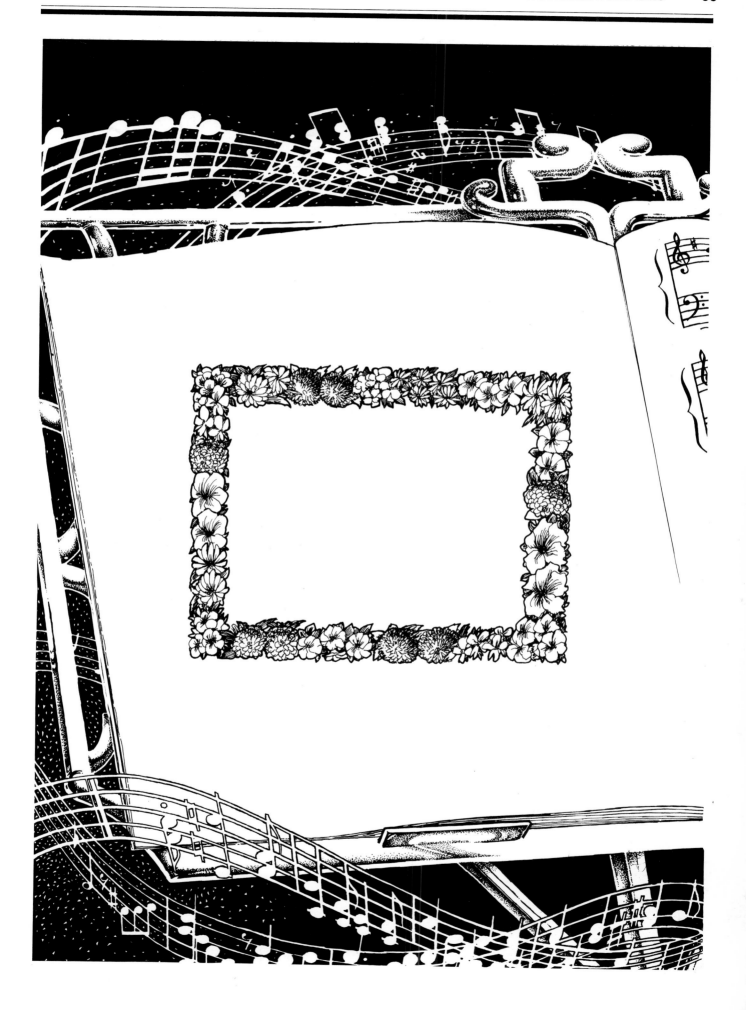

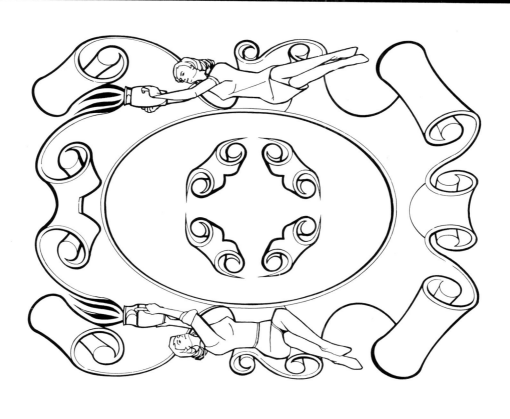

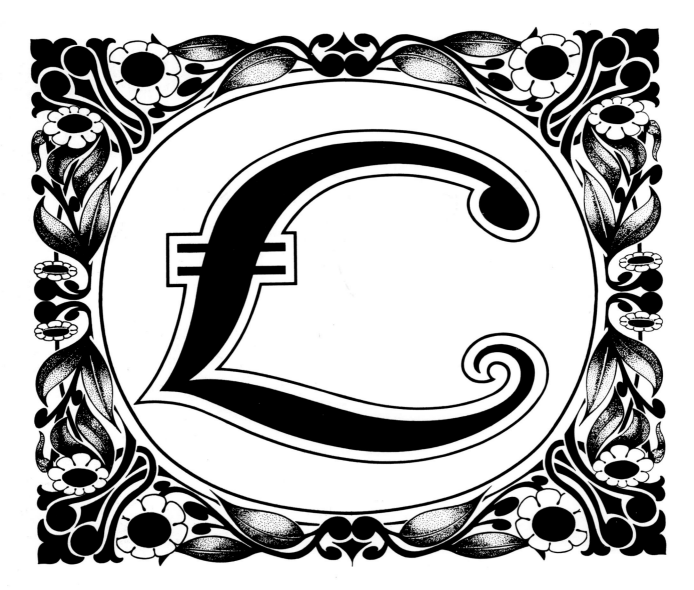

© Graphics World Ltd., England.

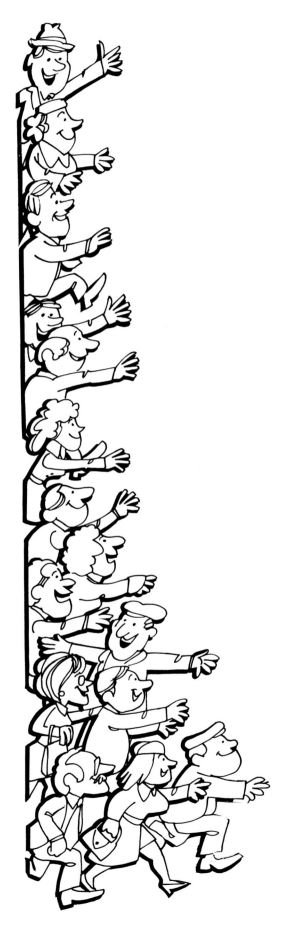

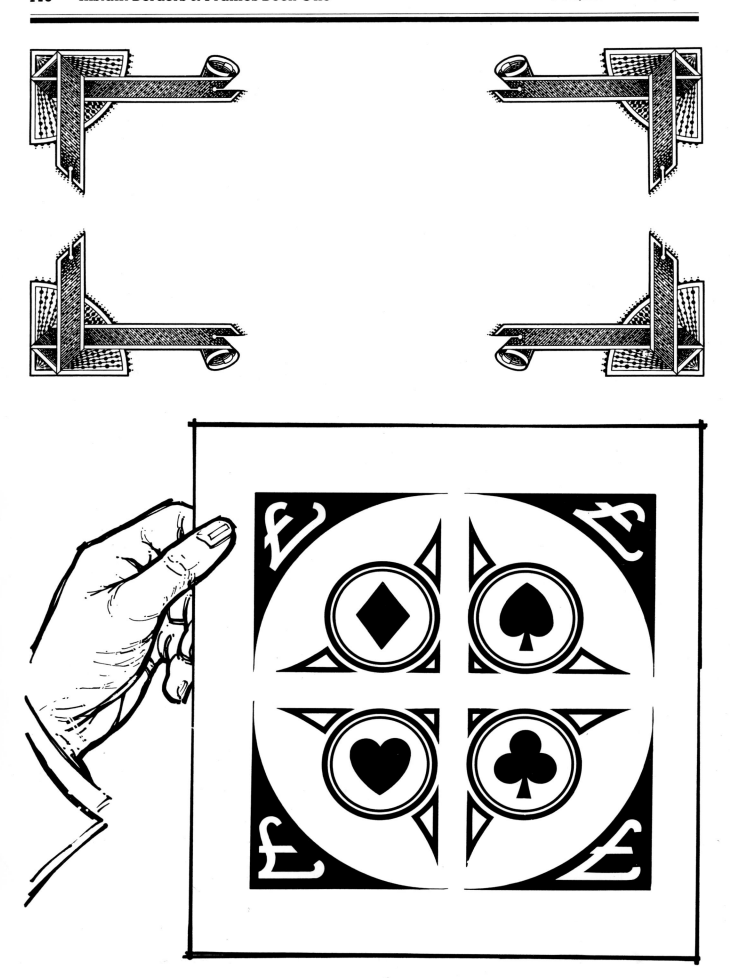

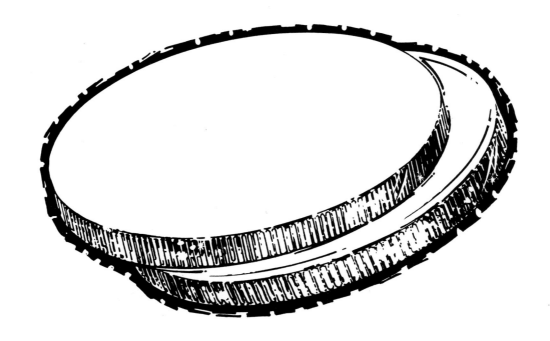

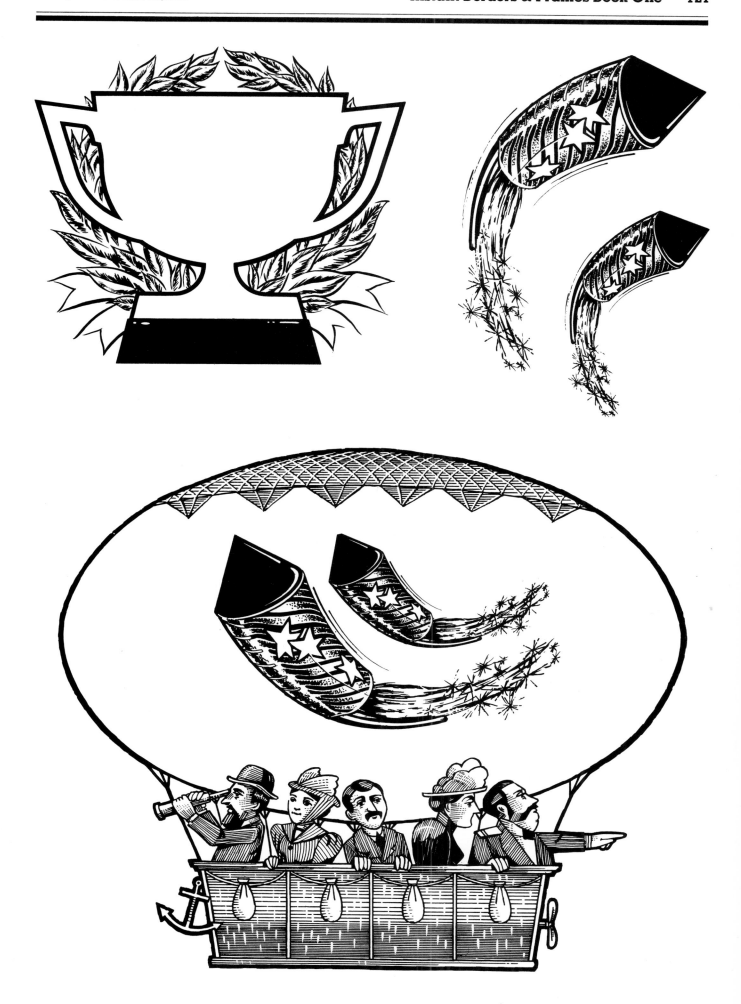

Safari Park

Carol
Service

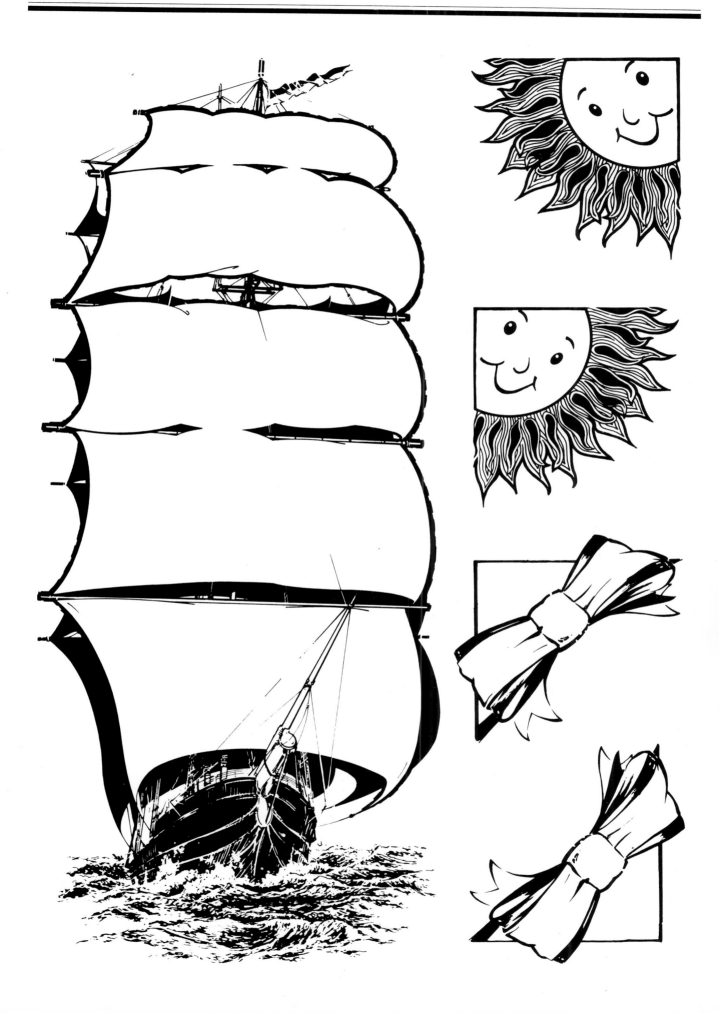

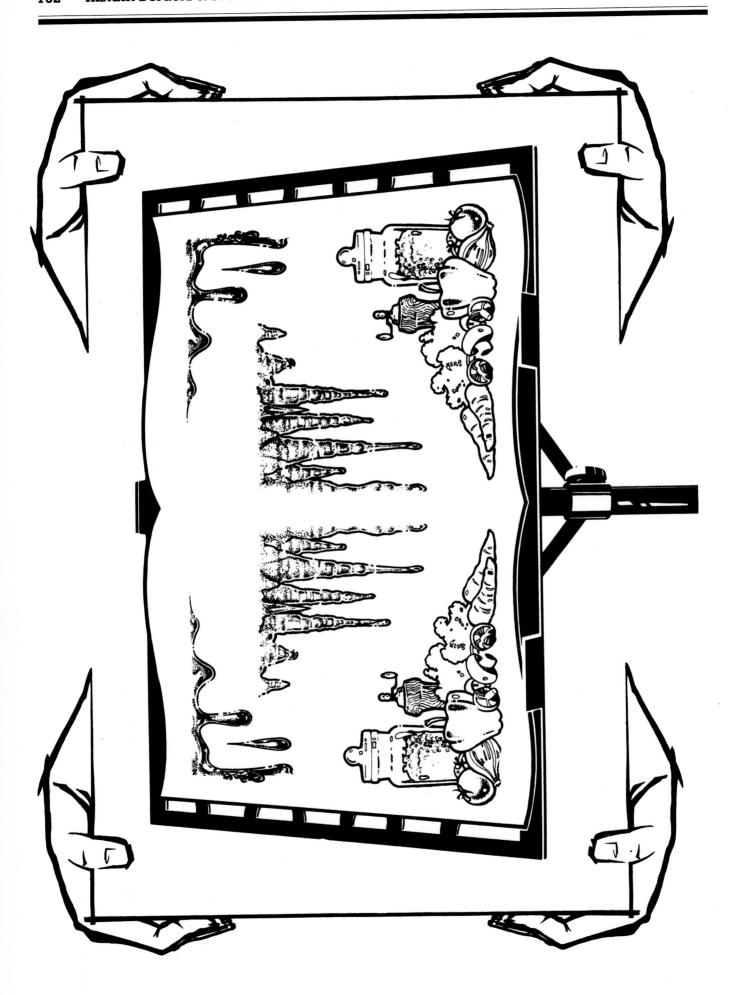

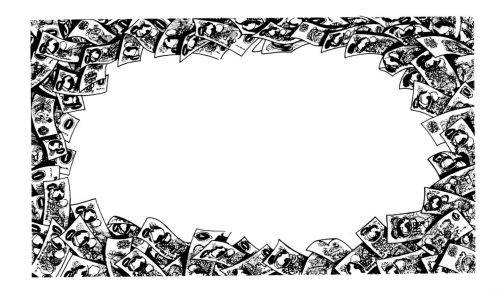

Check List

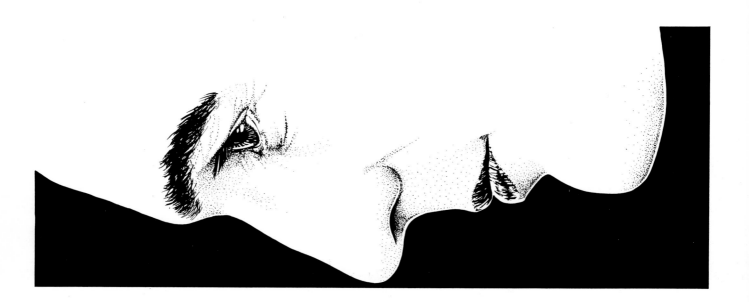

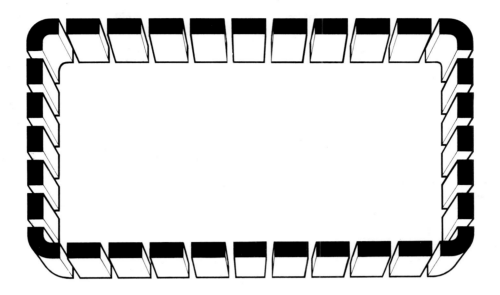

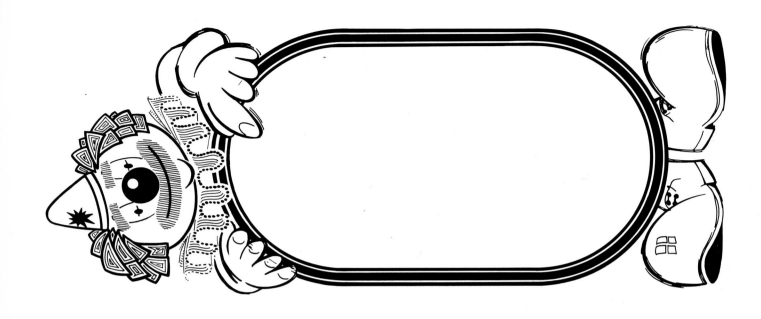

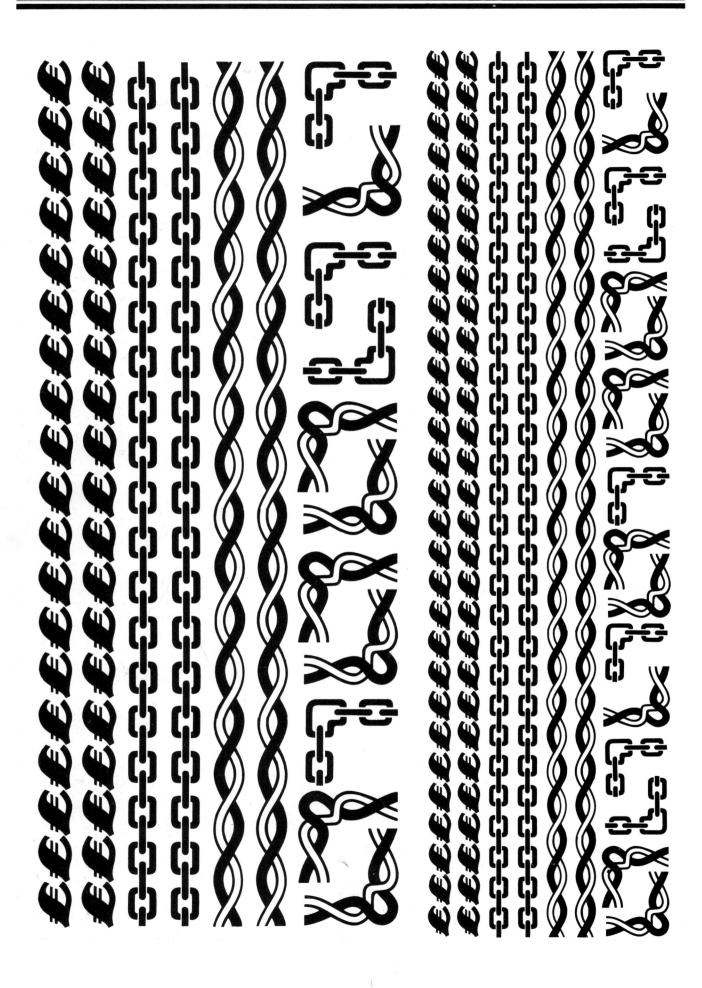

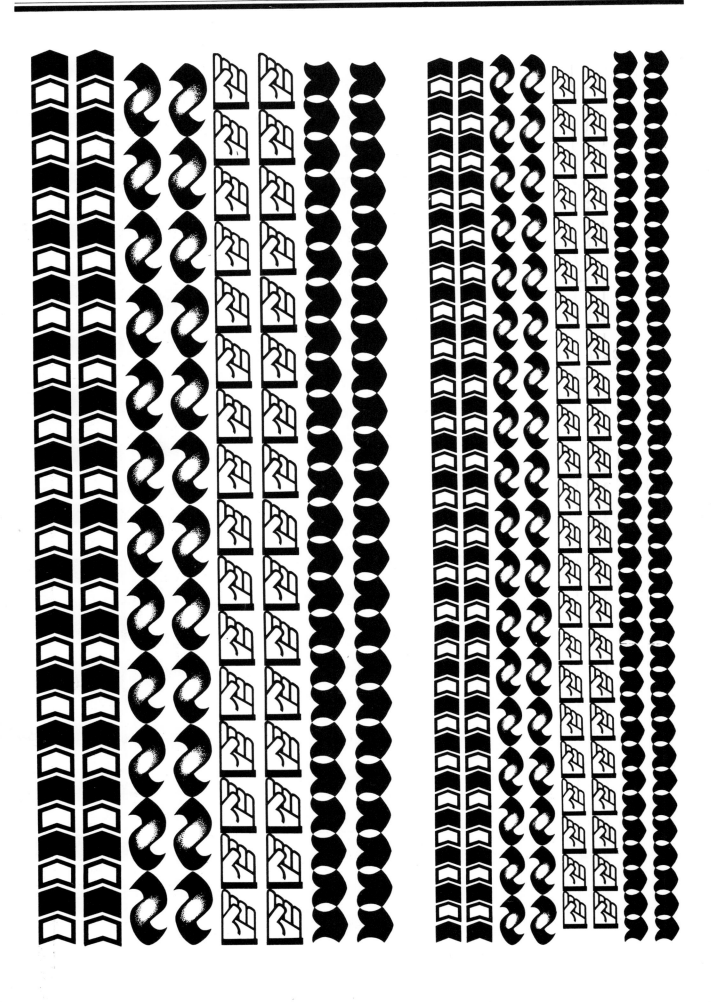

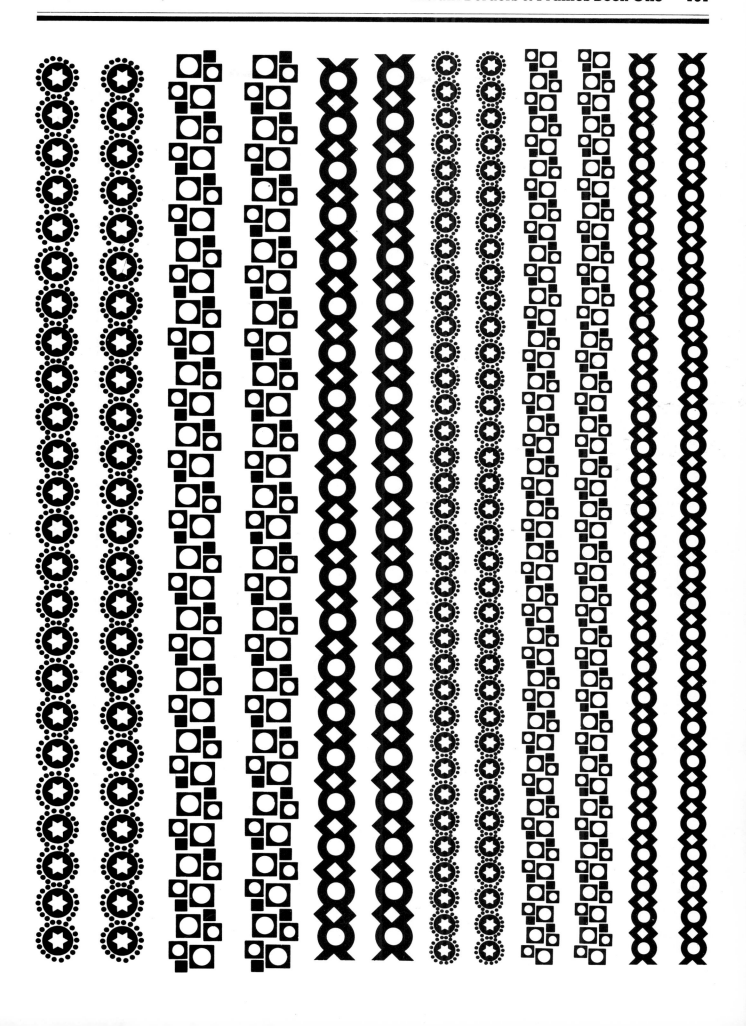

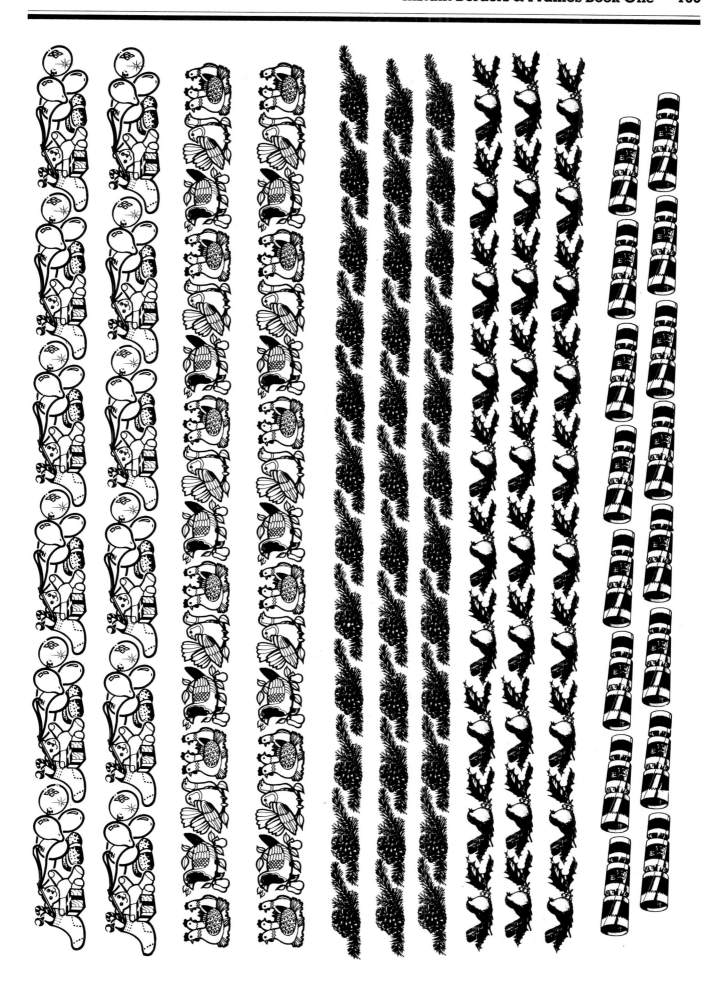

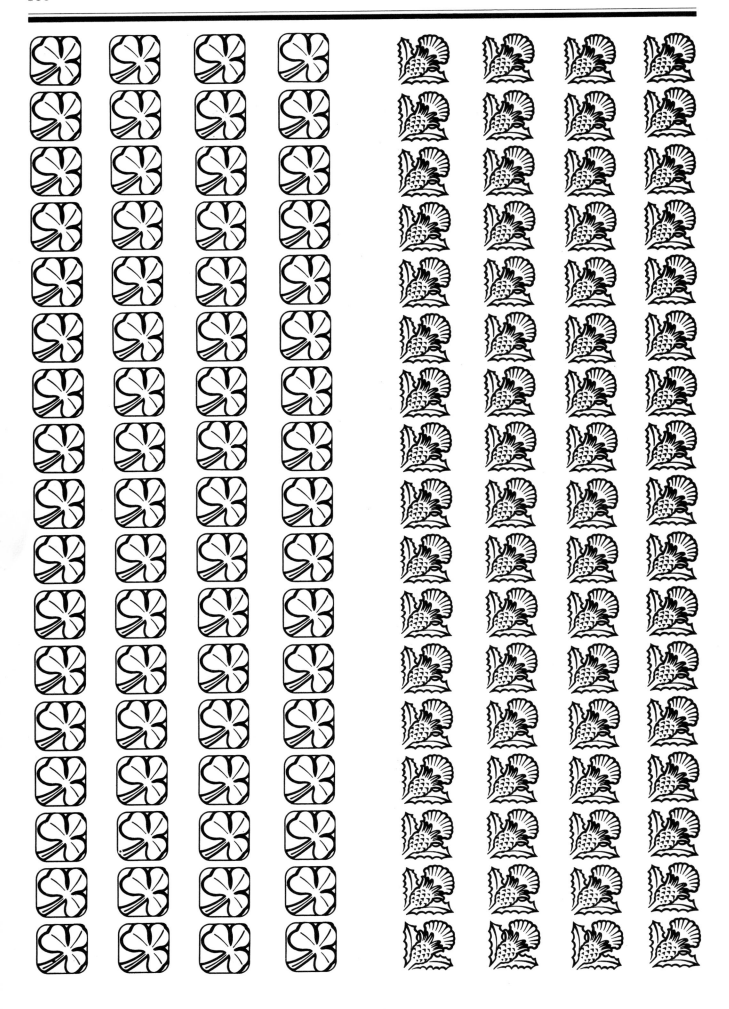

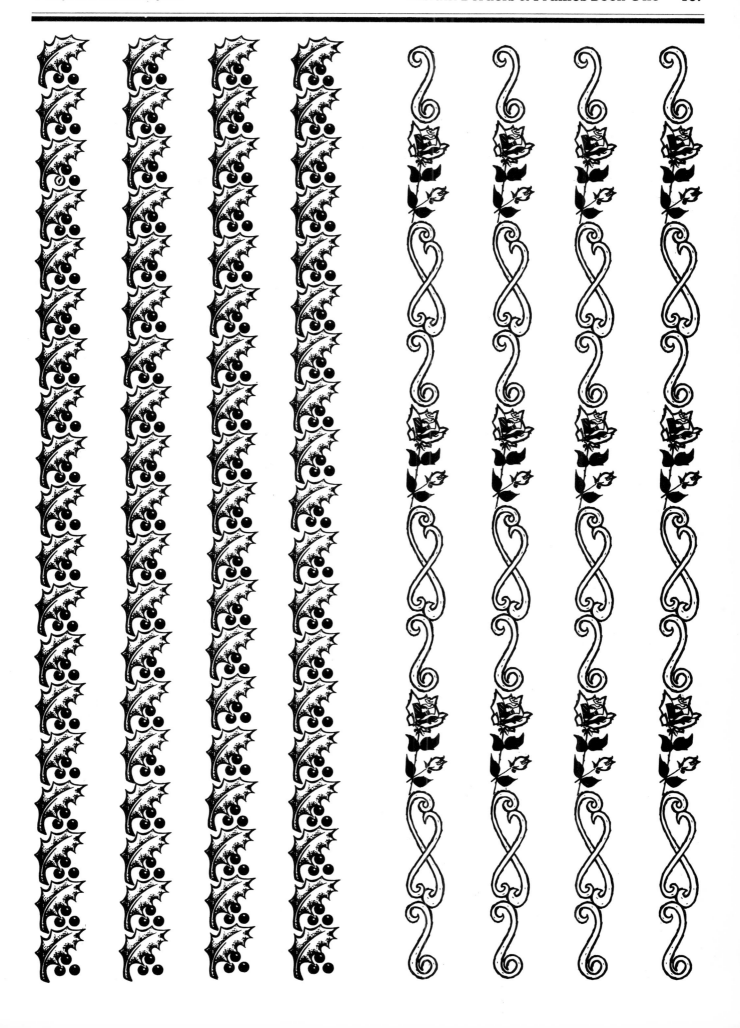

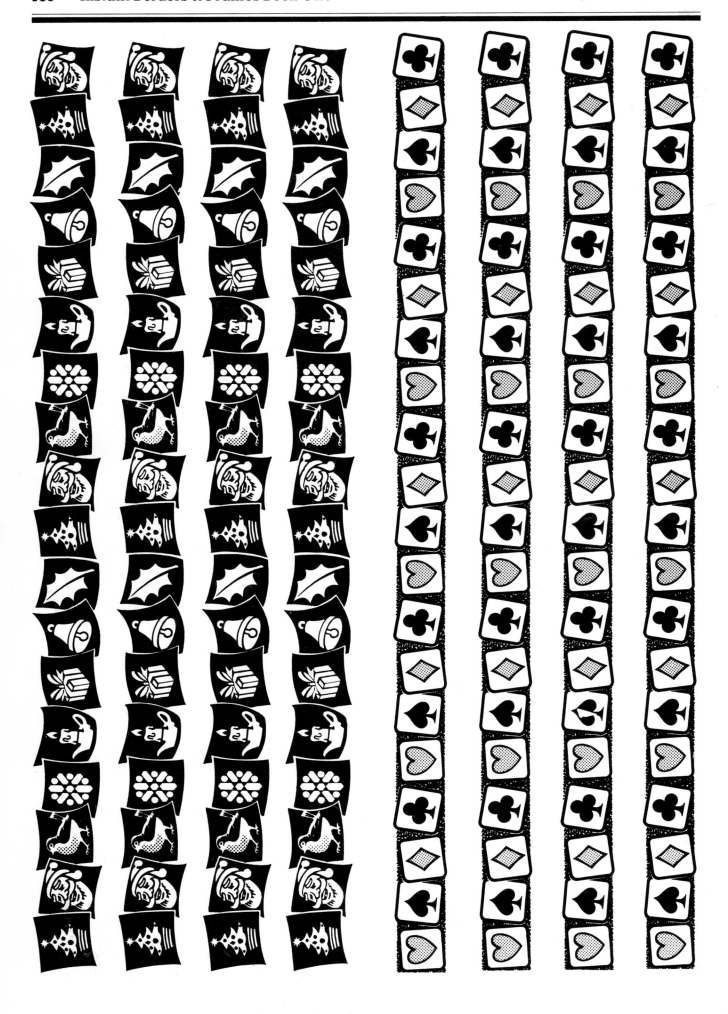

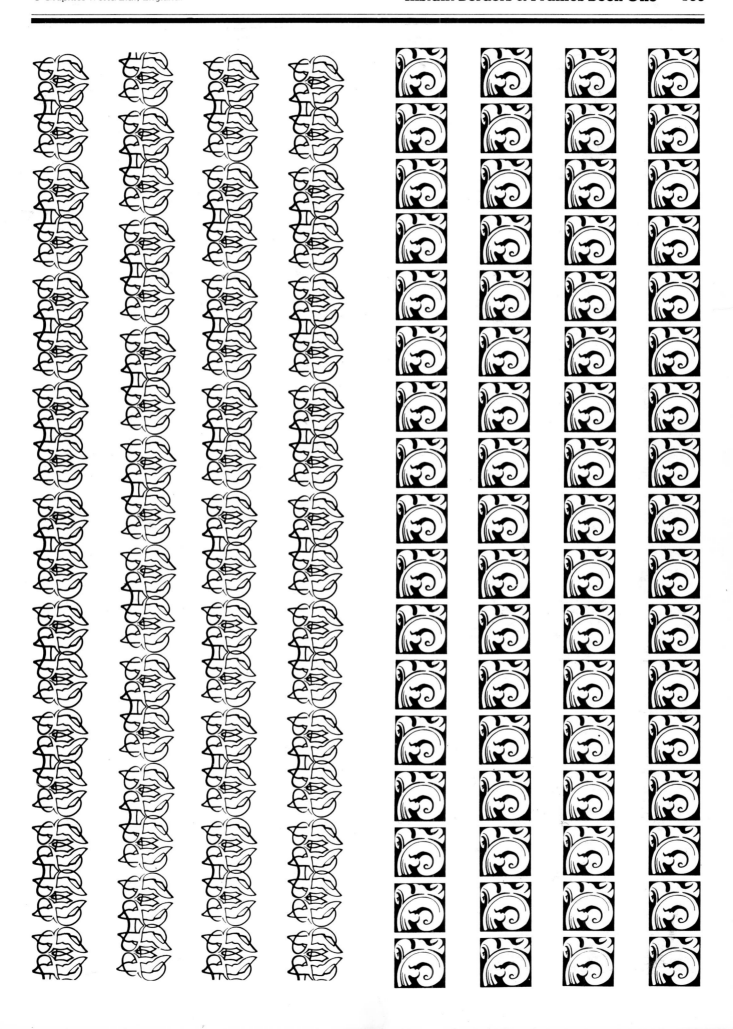

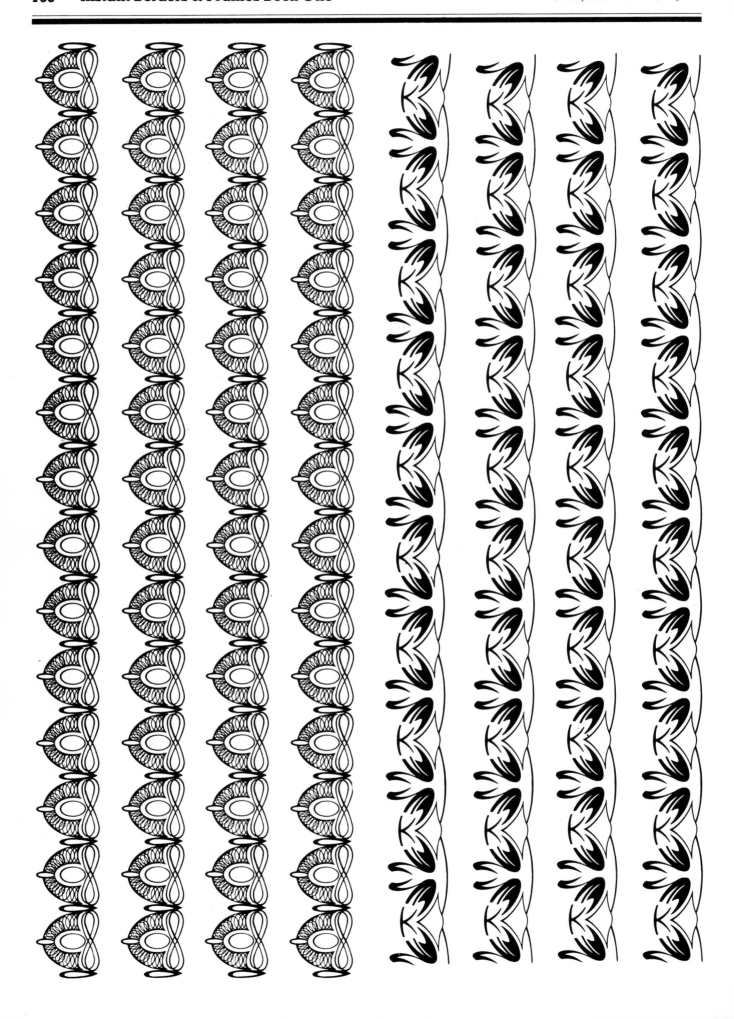

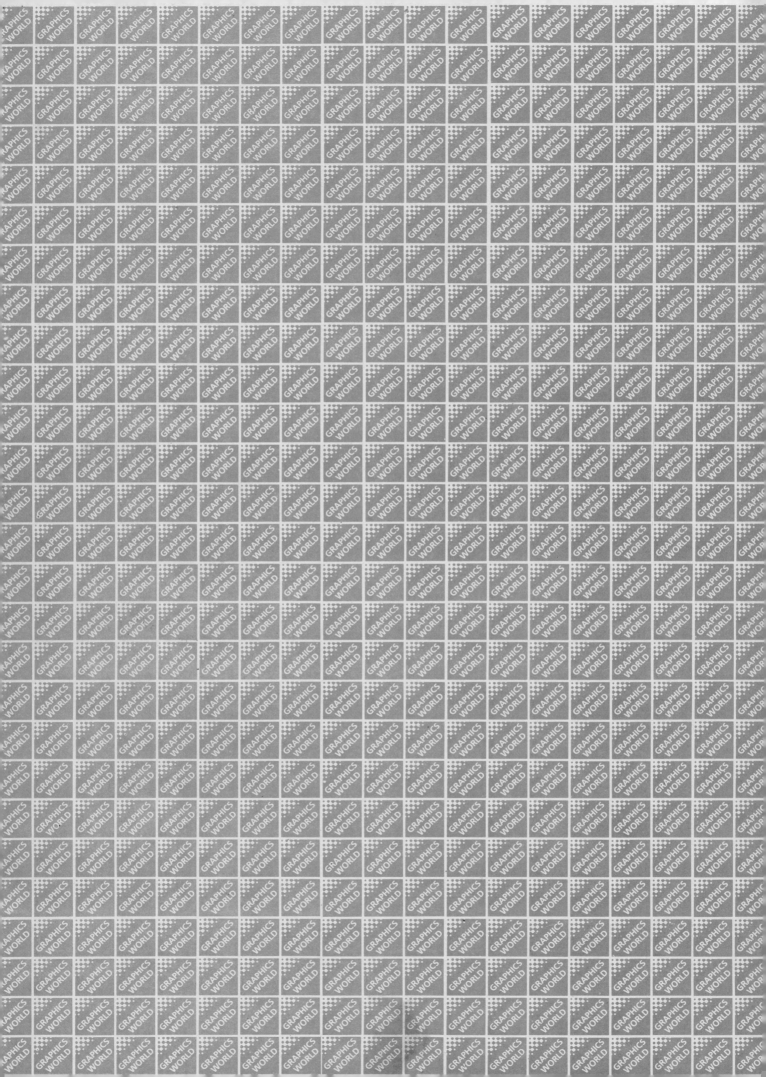